D1447692

TO THE MOON AND BACK:
LEADERSHIP REFLECTIONS FROM APOLLO

A SOCIAL AGE GUIDEBOOK

By Julian Stodd

CONTENTS

INTRODUCTION

Fifty years ago, the Apollo programme put a man on the Moon. Alongside the Manhattan Project, which had delivered the atomic bomb, it was probably the most complex and ambitious mobilisation of state and science the world has ever seen. It was a vast overreach of effort: achieving the aspiration required the invention and mastery of new technologies, alongside the systems of scheduling and control to use them. From project management to computer simulation, new disciplines emerged, and all of them in remarkably short order.

Apollo famously gave us Velcro[1], as well as a pen that can write in zero gravity[2], but much more too: it provides insight into humility and failure, the limits of political power, and exactly what we mean by *'the right stuff'*[3]. Apollo is a story told on many levels: on the one hand, the story of a nation, and an extension of the geopolitical struggle that nearly rained atomic fire on the world, and on the other, a very human story of complexity, risk, bravery, and determination, tragedy, alcoholism[4] and loss.

It is also a very human story of because, after a fifty-year hiatus of real purpose, we are at the start of a new chapter, heralded by an evolved relationship between state actors and the emergent Trans-Nationals, that is slashing the costs of launches and delivering on what was the hollow promise of legacy and reusability. The Moon, Mars and beyond all feel slightly more within our reach now.

The foundations of Apollo were in the literature: the dreamers, philosophers and pioneering science fiction writers who coalesced into the various rocketry societies, but it was the two world wars that lit the fuse. Rocketry was not

---

1   *This is an urban myth: it was invented by the Swiss in the 1940s.*

2   *This is another myth: they started to develop one, but the public got wind of it, and it was cancelled. So they just used pencils until someone else invented one.*

3   *The notion of 'The right stuff' was coined by Tom Wolfe as the title for his 1979 book about the Project Mercury astronauts.*

4   *Buzz Aldrin, the second man to walk on the moon, shares a very personal struggle with alcoholism, part of his life post Apollo. He was not the only astronaut to lose focus and purpose when the megalithic programme came to an end.*

specifically outlawed in Germany as part of the armistice in 1918 (while general weapon development was), largely because nobody could see the link. The risk was an development largely of the interwar years that therefore created a space for curiosity in a time of ambiguity, two factors that may provide the solution to much of the innovation crisis felt in established organisations today: it is the control over curiosity and almost pathological fear of curiosity that kills a learning culture, and leads directly to failure.

Of course, the Second World War provided a stimulus to deploy, and Von Braun's rockets did just that, hefting high explosives onto London, but even as the first V2 rockets took off, Von Braun saw it as not the end of a war, but the first step on the journey to the stars.

The end of the war saw the wholesale pillaging of technology and intact teams, with both Russia and the US racing for supremacy. The Apollo programme included at its heart the fully intact German military cadre and even some hardware.

If Apollo was anything, it was incremental: each successive launch mastered one new element in a complex interplay of technology and a complex power struggle against Russia, giving the whole thing a rather unusual dynamic. It was perfectly possible to be technologically superior but still to lose control of the narrative by simply being a few weeks too late. Sputnik, the first satellite that Russia lofted into orbit and that pinged its story of threat and fear into the heart of the US, demonstrated that with dynamic effect. Suddenly, distance collapsed.

The Saturn V rockets that delivered Apollo remain to this day among the most complex machines built by humans. And they are staggeringly powerful: the first minutes of launch unleashed the power of a nation through five thrusters.

It's easy to become lost in the hyperbole, but at its heart, Apollo was a human venture: the three astronauts who died consumed by fire on the launchpad in Apollo 1 died because of stupidity and arrogance, much as the Challenger astronauts did decades later. Technology cannot compete with the arrogance of control systems.

Every meta-narrative of Apollo can be broken down into micro-narratives: the ways that every component works together, the ways that problems were solved, the insights and revelations felt by the men who walked in space and on the surface of the Moon. I do believe that in its soul, the story of Apollo is one of fragility and humanity, and hence one that we can learn from, if not directly, then through reflection.

I've wanted to write about Apollo for some time, and as I filled a whole shelf in my library with various biographies, technical publications, and pulp fictions, about the programme, I became more daunted by the idea. The driving notion for me is that we can use a reflection upon the Apollo programme as the foundation of a broad reflection on leadership: it can form one of the lenses that I have talked about before, different ways of looking at the world. But it comes with the risk of being rubbish: the last thing I wanted to do was to draw crass lessons of leadership and bravery from Armstrong, Collins and Aldrin as they navigated the vacuum.

The Apollo Lander
July 20th
1969

© Julian Stodd

Instead, I have taken a rather selfish approach. At heart, the appeal for me is in the really rather fascinating details of the technology and programme: understanding the sequence and progression of development, learning something of the complexity and genius of the engineering, learning of some of the very human fallibilities and failings along the way and just enjoying the sheer magnitude and majesty of what may be the greatest adventure story ever told.

I'm sharing this in the format of one of my Social Age Guidebooks, which all work in a common format: they share what I hope is some interesting research and content, but also include sections that are my own attempt to draw out the meaning. In this case, I've written *'Leadership Reflections'* for each area. Mine may not be the same as yours, which is fine: they are shared simply as part of my own reflective journey.

CHAPTER 1:
ISOLATION

Michael Collins, piloting in the lunar orbiter Columbia, was, for a short time at least, the most isolated human in the universe. He orbited far from the Eagle, the spider-like lander that Neil Armstrong and Buzz Aldrin were piloting to the surface. He was farther still from the Earth, to which he remained intermittently connected through a long and fragile chain of communication[5] and the lonely tether of gravity. He was utterly alone on the dark side of the Moon.

July 20th, 1969, was the culmination of a journey measured in magnitudes: of money, of complexity, of risk, an archetypal pyramid project, with Armstrong's small step balanced on the pinnacle, but with over 400,000 others and decades of innovation, an almost inconceivable mass of experience, standing beneath.

Strange things happen in space: you get very little return for a great deal of effort, or, more accurately, it takes a very great deal of energy to direct a very small lander to the Sea of Tranquillity. To achieve this, Apollo 11 was not one spacecraft, but many stacked one atop the other: an assemblage of technologies, each of which would loft the Eagle one step closer to the magnificent desolation of the Moon[6] or drag it one step back towards the distant Earth.

---

5   Collins saw space flight as a 'long and fragile daisy chain of events' (Chaikin, 1994, p.189). All the early astronauts were pragmatists, raised through war, the test pilot mind-set (in which death was a frequent flier) and in which salvation came through preparedness, detail and possibly luck. It's interesting to note that while all were defined by technology, some turned to faith and art as responses to what they experienced.

6   While Armstrong's 'One small step' statement is the one immortalised as the words to describe the end of a journey, Aldrin's words 'magnificent desolation' more accurately describe where that journey took them (Aldrin, 2009, p. 34).

The first, second and third stages are the ones most familiar, as they are the ones we see discarded and falling back to Earth, but on top of them sat the Lunar Module, the Service Module and the Command Module, each in its own right powered and self-contained. It was not one rocket that blasted off from Cape Canaveral, but many: while the whole stack is called the Saturn V, there were five F-1 engines, mechanisms of demonic power, five J-2 engines, and further, smaller, engines, some of which were designed for multiple uses during the flight, right down to the tiny thrusters to control pitch and yaw or to direct discarded stages away from the main stack—in all, over eighty of them.

This complexity involves a dance, or rather, several dances: the Lunar Module, Command Module, and Service Module, each separating and re-engaging multiple times because the order in which they were stacked was not the order in which they were used: a Tetris puzzle of incredible complexity, carried out while hurtling along at over 11km/second— almost twenty-five thousand miles per hour. That sounds dramatic until we remember that speed is relative: with both vessels travelling at that speed, the dance appears slow and stately from the relative position of each observer, a fact that belies the truth that the astronauts still hold the record for the fastest speed attained by a human.

Only two of the three Apollo astronauts would land on the Moon. Collins remained behind in his lonely orbit, piloting the Command Module/Service Module mashup (those two mated modules forming Columbia while the Eagle, which had flown protected between the first three stages and the final two, could depart and start its dangerous descent.

The Eagle detached with the push of a button by Collins in the Command Module: a final earthly act, pitching it to the Moon, like the most expensive baseball in history. With that push came a change of perspective: *'I think you've got a fine looking machine, there, Eagle'*, said Collins, as Armstrong jockeyed the lander into a stable position, flying alongside[7], *'despite the fact that you're upside down'*. *'Somebody's upside down'*, retorted Armstrong, revealing a truism of perspective: it's always measured from our own.

---

7   *In Chaikin (1994), p.189.*

In space, there is no true *'up'*, except that which we choose to adopt, meaning that a spacecraft can make use of all interior surfaces with impudent abandon, or at least it can until the time comes to land or it gets too near to another source of gravity. When separated, though, Eagle and Columbia manoeuvred, and in doing so, gave each other a relative position of upside-down-ness.

It may seem trivial, but relative position is important, something that Oliver Morton[8] explores in his fascinating exposition on the iconic *'Earthrise'* photo, arguably the most famous (and certainly one of the most significant) photos in history. It's the one that shows the vibrant *'blue marble'* rising over that magnificent dereliction—except that it didn't used to.

When first presented to the press, it was positioned with the Moon's surface as a wall on the right, and the Earth suspended in space on the left (a framing that Morton reminds us was parodied by George Lucas when he had the Death Star drift into view around the planet Yavin nine years later). It was only when it landed on the cover of Time magazine that it took the more familiar Earthrise posture (possibly shadowing the framing used by Stanley Kubrick in 2001: A Space Odyssey a year earlier). It is an interesting intertwining of cultural drivers, with cinema both responding to, and shaping, the dominant narrative. We all believe that we stand on top of the earth: none of us feel that we are on the side.

So there stands Collins, orbiting the Moon, alone, while Armstrong and Aldrin kick up the dust (dust that would permeate every crevice of the lander with its glassy consistency and gunpowder smell as it reacted with the oxygen inside), at the end of his daisy chain: the most isolated man that there has ever been.

---

8   *Morton's book provides a delightful perspective from both scientific and aesthetic viewpoints, rambling from mythology to gravity and back again. It's a really neat reflective addition to the literature. As a side note, I read it as my first book while on paternity leave, so I consumed it in two-page 'moments' snatched alongside my gently snoring, or wildly screaming, son..*

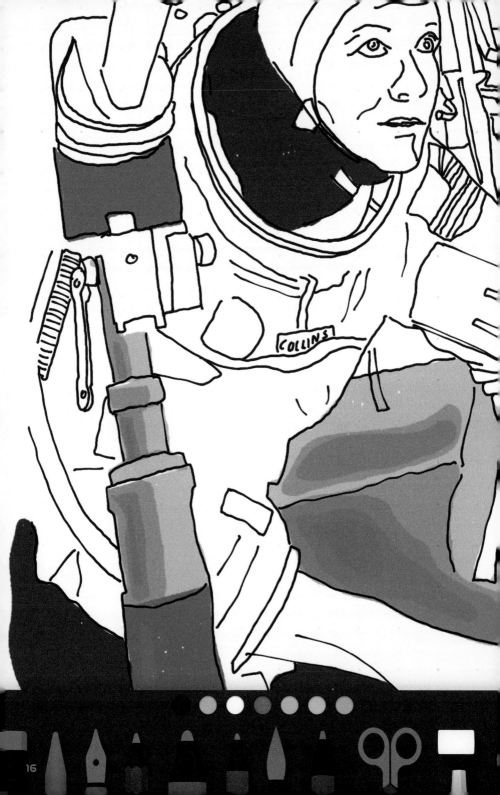

LEADERSHIP REFLECTIONS

1.   The Apollo programme was a statement of national power and pride, but the ultimate expression of it was validated by a single man, thrown from the Earth by thunder, hung upon a gossamer thread. **Impact is not always about thunder, but sometimes about fragility.**

2.   One lens through which to view this is that of perspective: from the Earth, Collins was almost forgotten, outshone by the men on the Moon. For Collins, his *'world'* shifted to his craft and his companions on the Moon that, by size, dominated his view. Earth receded to a marble: this is a legacy of Apollo, that our atmosphere is made visible in the vastness of space, its fragility exposed. **But sometimes that which is closest dominates our view.**

3.   While the Eagle and Columbia moved only a few metres apart, their perspectives flipped, to the point at which one was upside down. How often does this happen, even in terrestrial divergence? **It does not take much distance to create an uncrossable divide.**

NOTES:

CHAPTER 2:
ORBIT

If you are a mathematician or orbital mechanic, please feel free to skip this section. But for the rest of us amateurs, consider falling down. Or rather, falling off.

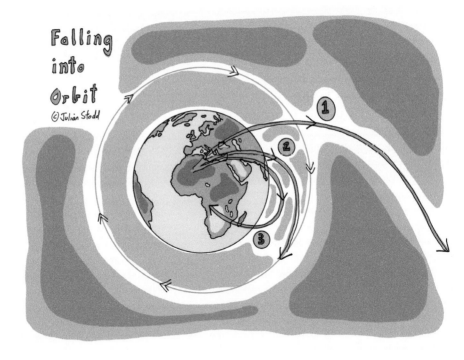

One thing I learned while researching this book that stuck in my head: that going *'into orbit'* is not about throwing something up into the air and hoping that it stays there, but more about throwing it in a curve, off the edge, until it perpetually falls.

There are two forces at play: the energy spent in lobbing the spacecraft up and the gravity that tries to pull it down again. If you throw a ball on Earth, it goes in an arc: you put energy into the system, and the ball goes up, but over time and distance, gravity pulls it back down. Literally, *'what goes up must come down'* [9].

However, that is not always true: if you put enough energy into throwing it, it could break away from the Earth and keep going forever, or until it hits a passing spaceship, alien or interplanetary greenhouse. It takes a lot of energy, but then space travel is mainly about energy, and escaping our planet's gravity is a big part of it.

The diagram shows the three states that I found most useful to understand this: launch the spaceship with not enough energy, and you get a ballistic lob [3] (which is pretty much how an intercontinental ballistic missile works). What goes up travels in an arc and then comes down, with a bang. This is good if you are trying to hit something, but bad if you want to get into orbit.

Use more energy, and the spaceship goes up, escapes gravity, and goes forever [1]. But use just the right amount, and it goes up in an arc and starts to fall down, but it's gone *'over the edge'* [2].

It remains in balance: it is, in effect, endlessly falling. In my understanding, it misses the edge of the planet and so falls, but as it travels around the planet, gravity goes with it, pulling on it equally at any point.

Once in orbit, it takes relatively little energy to maintain it, which probably speaks to the stability of many systems.

---

9   *And yes, I know there is friction and energy leaking out as noise and heat, but let's keep it simple.*

LEADERSHIP
REFLECTIONS

1. It may require a great deal of brute force to achieve an end, **but the devil is in the details.**

2. Understanding the complex forces and interplay of forces at work and **fine-tuning with a nudge in the right direction** is probably the route to success.

NOTES:

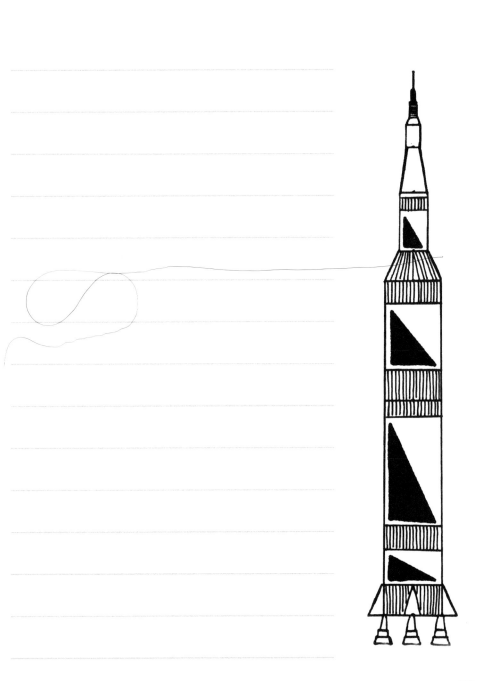

CHAPTER 3:
STORYTELLING

'*Oh my God, look at that picture over there*', called out Bill Anders, crew member of Apollo 8. '*What is is?*' asked Frank Borman, the mission commander. '*The Earth coming up. Wow, is that pretty!*'[10]

Earthrise
© Julian Stodd

Apollo was distinguished from earlier forms of exploration by the depth, synchronicity and range of its documentation: live TV streaming the key moments of the voyage, a full range of both colour and black and white photography, shaky home movies shot from the surface of the Moon. Apollo had it all. You can read the full mission radio transcripts, if you have the

---

10   *Chaikin (1994), p. 112.*

time, or listen to the audio to get close to the original conversations (and tensions). There's even a contemporary Twitter account *'live'* recasting the Apollo 11 mission word for word for the 50th anniversary.

As a storytelling activity, Apollo works on many levels: it's a story of national struggle and pride, the story of communism versus capitalism, the story of Kennedy, the playboy prince, versus the evil empire (with the fear generated by Sputnik as its genesis). It's a story of technology over nature, a story about conquest and exploration, a narrative about progress and the triumph of the 20th century.

At a different level, it's a story about the *'little guy'*, the 400,000 men and women who worked on individual rivets, pipes, stitches, fluids, calculations, and gambles that carried three men to the Moon. That story is one of individual connection: the interconnectivity of the system, the way that everyone can see how the smallest of cogs drives the largest of machines. That story is also one of subservience and obedience, blind faith and fervour.

At the most human level, it's a blue-eyed myth of three American boys, back from the war, off to space: their steely strength, and stoical bravery, their occasional sacrifice. It's a story for everyone, as long as everyone is white, middle-aged and male[11].

There was a parallel narrative about racial inequality and the colour blindness of the whole programme, but at least at the start, there was very little conversation about an African American astronaut. The White House was aware that the story of a black astronaut would be a big political win and did put some pressure on NASA, even ensuring that there was a black candidate in the test pilot programme[12] (the feedstock for astronaut training in the early days), but when he washed out, little fuss was made. It would be 1983 before the first African American astronaut went up on the shuttle, the same year that the first American female one went[13].

---

11 *In private tests, women were show to be just as capable as the men, but that was not part of the dominant narrative of the time. Instead, their role was relegated to the now famous 'calculators' and seamstresses who stitched the space suits (Morton, 2019).*

12 *Morton (2019), p. 110.*

13 *Twenty years after the first Russian cosmonaut had flown.*

When we examine the relics of Apollo, there is a clear divide between the epic and the mundane: photos of the behemoth Saturn V boosters, steaming and venting as they snort and stamp their hooves on the launch pad, the sight of American aluminium and gold foil starlit against the Earth, the titanic-blank-visored astronauts standing legs akimbo on the Moon, but also photos of carefully documented chicken curry, condoms for taking a pee and the graffiti that adorned the interior of the Columbia Command Module[14]. Some photos have value without context, and others seem desperate to provide context to the everyday banality of bodily functions.

One of the most famous photos is that of the first footprint on the Moon, although the reality is a little more prosaic: often assumed to be that first step

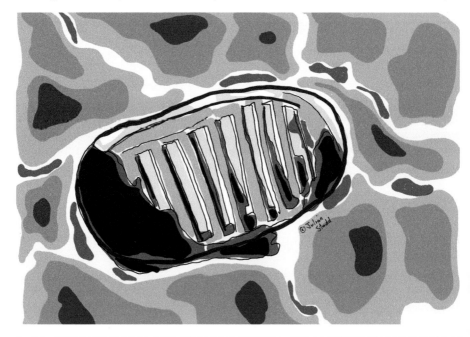

---

14   Apollo 13 is the famous failed mission, when an explosion crippled the Service Module, necessitating using the Lunar Lander as a lifeboat. Before re-entering the Earth's atmosphere, it was necessary to jettison this lifeboat, but clearly not while anyone was still on board. One of my favourite Apollo 13 anecdotes concerned one of the astronauts, exhausted and concerned, taping over the 'jettison' button for the 'lifeboat' a note along the lines of 'do not press this button', worried that despite all the technology, training, and know-how, he would accidentally resort to routine and press it. I'm unable to locate the source of this anecdote at this time, but Lovell's and Kluger's definitive account is a great resource. Columbia's graffiti is discussed in Muir-Harmony (2018).

taken by Armstrong, the photo is actually one of Aldrin's steps, taken not for the historical record, but rather as a series of photos to document the properties of the lunar soil: they were intended to assist the technicians in establishing future designs for Moon boots, vehicles and even buildings, as well as enabling them to estimate maximum walking and driving speeds[15]. We now assign the photo totemic value: it represents the first step, the claim, the planted flag.

To some, Apollo 11 represents the start of the Anthropocene, the *'Age of Humans'*, a description of a new epoch, characterised by the time that the dominant forces at play on the face of the Earth are human in origin. In this instance, the first step on the Moon both polluted, claimed and changed the eternal[16].

But Apollo 11 was not a story in isolation: the ten years of its conception and execution spanned the summer of love, the Vietnam War and an evolving political context. Since Armstrong first set foot upon the Moon, the human population of planet Earth has doubled. War, famine and strife seem eternal. And we have retreated from the Moon.

The story of Apollo seems more a historical anachronism in some ways, possibly a morality play. Certainly it holds very little of the contemporary in its stride: most modern references are along the lines of how much faster/more powerful computing is now or how wasteful those government programmes of old were.

'Hey, don't take that, it's not scheduled', said Borman, as Anders lined up to snap the Earth. As with everything on Apollo, the sequence of shots that would be taken, every frame, were planned and documented, and an idle aesthetic of the Earth was not part of the photo plan.

'Hand me that roll of colour, quick, would you?', said Anders, urgently. '*You got it? Take several of them'*, urged Jim Lovell, the third Apollo 8 crew member.

Some stories need to be told, sometimes we have to deviate from a plan and sometimes you have to go with your heart. Similarly, some stories only find value in hindsight: you cannot plan for future relevance, and you cannot control an evolving narrative.

---

15   *Mailer (2009).*
16   *Extended debate in Morton (2019).*

LEADERSHIP REFLECTIONS

1. **Stories are contextualised and re-contextualised in ways that move beyond our control:** even our formal relics of discourse can be judged and reshaped in evolving contexts.

2. **An authenticity of action is the best guarantee of longevity.**

3. **Even a seemingly indomitable narrative of power can be usurped by evolving social contexts:** the role of women and African Americans in the space programme provides a clear example.

4. **A story, no matter its wealth and might, can be felled by authentic truths.**

5. Stories operate on multiple levels, from the individual up to the organisational, and national. Each level may hold a different truth, and **some may be held in opposition to the others.**

6. Leadership is not simply about telling our own story: it's about **enabling others to shape and share theirs.**

NOTES:

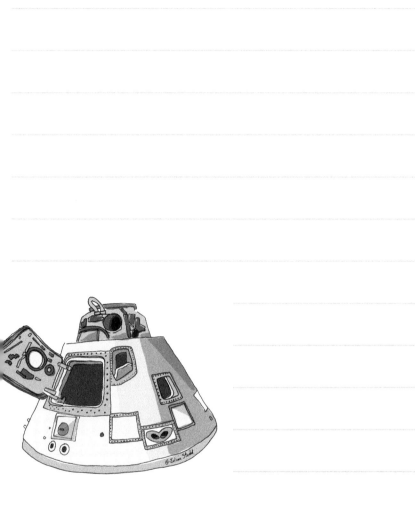

CHAPTER 4:
ULLAGE

As everyone knows from his or her schooldays understanding of rockets, they come in stages: during launch, each successive stage is used up and separated. When this separation occurs, it's not as smooth as you may think: when one rocket stops burning, the craft brakes and can momentarily become weightless. Then the next stage engine kicks in, and off you go again.

But in the complex world of fuel, this is an issue: weightlessness means that the fuel may not be at the bottom of the tank, where you need it. It sloshes up to the top, where it does no good at all. And as with most things rocketry, this is very bad news.

So as well as the giant Saturn V engines and the ascent and descent SR1 engines, there was a whole series of ullage rockets with a small but important function: they started to fire one-fifth of a second before the stage separated, fired for a total of four seconds, and then were discarded thirty seconds later. They served two purposes: firstly, they forced any gas into the space at the top of the fuel tank, where it belonged, and secondly, they created a slight pressure at the engine inlet.

Saturn V rockets carried at least four of these engines, with 150kg of solid rocket propellant in each, and they served a small but vital function in the success of the mission[17].

---

17   Woods (2016).

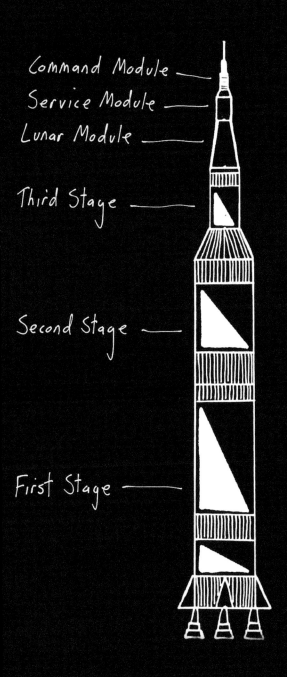

Command Module ———

Service Module ———

Lunar Module ———

Third Stage ———

Second Stage ———

First Stage ———

The Saturn V
Launch Vehicle

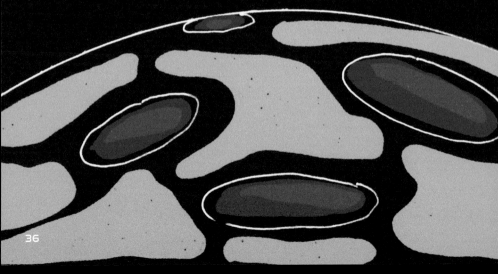

36

LEADERSHIP REFLECTIONS

1.   Small cogs make the whole machine work.

NOTES:

CHAPTER 5:
FAILURE, COMPLEXITY AND CONTROL

Failure Is Not an Option is the title of Gene Kranz's book, a comprehensive overview of Mission Control from its inception through his time as flight director. Today, it is a rather jaded expression: more a machismo assertion of power than a guiding principle, worn by its application in contexts that do not justify it or to systems that can never guarantee it. Failure is always an option, possibly the default one.

© Julian Stodd

Of course, in one of those narrative ironies, Kranz never used the phrase himself: it was written by the screenwriters for the Apollo 13 film, and it sounded so good that Kranz made the fictitious words that he never uttered his own[18].

But even if he never used the words, the statement reflected a real mind-set of the time. Mission Control was built around a new paradigm: an approach of systematised problem-solving and connected knowledge hitherto unknown. It's one of the most fascinating aspects of Apollo: the way that they had to invent the rocket and invent the systems of oversight and control to actually use it.

Before it, the Manhattan Project had tamed, then unleashed, the power of the atom bomb: a programme of great complexity and secrecy, with the ultimate aim to take life away. Apollo worked on a different scale in both directions: it needed more people to design and build it, but it aimed only to affect three people as a result. And it was designed to keep them alive[19].

When the Saturn V rocket launched, it had the potential to detonate with one-twenty-sixth the power of the atomic bomb that destroyed Hiroshima: a not inconsiderable challenge to life and limb if you sat atop it[20].

Assuming the craft survived launch, a mission to the Moon may last a number of weeks. During all that time, there was the constant need to monitor systems, identify and mitigate risks, dynamically adapt the schedule and react to emergent issues, be they human or mechanical.

Travelling on Earth is risky because of dangers that turn up and kill us, but broadly, the default state is life: to starve, dehydrate, or succumb to

---

18   In https://en.m.wikipedia.org/wiki/Gene_Kranz, retrieved 26 July 2019.

19   The Manhattan Project [https://en.m.wikipedia.org/wiki/Manhattan_Project] employed an estimated 130,000 people, while Apollo is reckoned to have taken over 400,000 [https://en.m.wikipedia.org/wiki/Apollo_program] (retrieved 26 July 2019).

20   To create a safety margin around the Apollo launches, the two launch pads were situated in a remote area, surrounded by marshland and far from habitation. Even so, had a rocket detonated on the pad, it would have created a significant crater. Studies were carried out to ascertain just how large, predominantly to inform the design of the escape system intended to carry the Command Module away from the inferno in the event of catastrophic failure. By their own admission, the authors of the final report stated that much of their work was based on calculated guesses (Day, 2006). In the dynamic context of an exploding rocket, there were just too many variables at play.

illness usually takes time. Life can be lost suddenly to accidents, but even then there is a chance of extraction or treatment for broken limbs. Beyond the limits of our atmosphere, the default state is death, with no prospect of rescue or resuscitation. Any leak, mechanical failure, one single wrong decision can instantly cause a disaster. Space is very unforgiving.

In such situations, we rely on protective systems. The technology of Apollo can, in that sense, be seen in two contexts. The first is transport, to get us to the Moon and back, with the various permutations of craft and staged launch. The second is to preserve life through life support systems (when things are going well), and emergency protocols (to recover when they don't). Apollo can thus be seen as a project that lofted a small bubble of our earth's atmosphere safely to the Moon and retrieved it days later. The entire programme represents a series of connected, and nested, bubbles. Space suits themselves are small space ships, capable of preserving life.

Gene Kranz, as flight director, was responsible for the systems that facilitated both those ends: to successfully propel three men to the Moon and back and to ensure they stayed alive while making the journey. Doing so meant inventing an entire discipline of Mission Control.

While images of the control centre show lines of desks and serried ranks of white-shirted men, the reality for the astronauts in the Command Module was somewhat different: for them, it was largely a conversation with a friend.

The hierarchy of Mission Control relied on principles of specialism (experts on hand), aggregation (the interaction between disciplines: combinant effects), filtering (signal from noise and both the timeliness and relevance to the matter at hand[21]), structured decision-making (reporting lines that accounted for dependencies and causality in the days before computers could do this) and flow (the right knowledge or decision points in the right hands and between disciplines: combinant effects)

---

21   Apollo 13, the story told in the Tom Hanks film of the same name, reflected this in great detail: not all problems were solved at once, but rather the most critical for life were solved first, despite not knowing if subsequent issues were solvable at all. One of the most interesting observations is how some factors were just accepted as risk, e.g. the SR1 motor that would lift from the Moon had no backup, hence no contingency, and hence could not be modelled for anything other than a success or failure state.

The entire apparatus was intended to funnel down to two individuals: the flight director and the capsule communicator (CAPCOM). The flight director made the calls, and the CAPCOM was the only person who routinely could speak to the astronauts. There was no free-for-all, no cluttered radio chatter, but rather one voice, and a voice that they could trust.

The CAPCOM was typically a fellow astronaut, maybe from the backup team, who would have trained alongside the men in space and who would know what they needed, what they were feeling and how to convey complex information fast, but with empathy. Sometimes the role of CAPCOM was to know what not to ask: the astronauts were superb, but not super-human. Sometimes they got tired, annoyed, frustrated, probably even scared. In these times, the CAPCOM had his finger on the balance of the scales.

If the flight director sat at the centre of the web, with the CAPCOM by his side, the lines that radiated out represented each unique function, or specialism, that was needed to launch and retrieve the capsule. Each line, each individual, was referred to by his[22] acronym[23], so to listen to the recordings of the missions is to hear a terse to-and-fro, peppered by the jargon and terminology that enabled efficiency and accuracy in flow.

- CONTROL was a Lunar Module engineer, with responsibility for propulsion, abort guidance, navigation and the on-board computers.

- EECOM was responsible for electrical, environmental, communications, cryogenic, fuel cells, pyrotechnic and structural systems.

- FIDO was the flight dynamics officer who specialised in launch and orbit trajectories (which might dynamically change as issues emerged).

- FOD was the flight operations director.

- GNC looked after guidance, navigation and control systems for altitude, as well as aspects of computer hardware.

---

22   *My editor encouraged me to change this to 'his or her', but to my knowledge, the section heads were all men, so i've stuck with it. There are well documented examples of the women who acted as 'computers', as well as certain other roles.*
22   *Definitions and roles derived from Kranz (2000).*

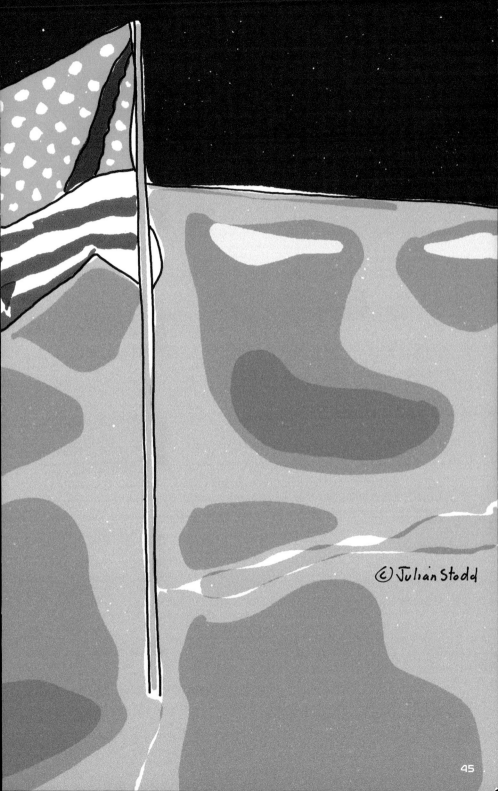

©Julian Stodd

45

- GUIDO was a specialist in navigation and software.

- INCO looked after instrumentation, communications, command and the live television systems for the Command Module, Lunar Module, any extra vehicular activities and the Lunar Rover in later missions.

- PAO was the public affairs officer whose whole job was to filter and release information to the press and public.

- RETRO, the retrofire officer, specialised in the final re-entry trajectories for return.

- SimSup led the training team that tested both astronauts, and the entire Mission Control team, to the limit.

- SPAN, the spacecraft analysis team, could access the broader design and manufacturing teams spread around the country.

It's worth noting that many of the men who held these positions were in their early twenties, literally making up the rules as they went.
Kranz described how when he joined the precursor Mercury programme, he was tasked with creating the mission rules and training approaches, which simply did not exist. It was a monumental effort, equal to the technology taking shape in the laboratories and through a series of conflagrations on the launch pads.

Manned space flight is just that: manned by the men in the capsule and the men (and a very few women) in Mission Control and beyond.

From inception, NASA was military in approach, but civilian in operation. Certainly many people fell out of assorted aviation programmes to land at NASA, but when they got there, they were thrust into new jobs in new disciplines. Apollo was all about learning.

Space flight is risky, but success does not lie in avoiding, or mitigating, all the risk: it's typically about understanding how risk flows and, critically, cascades. When does one failure lead to another, and when does it sit in isolation? When is one failure acceptable, and when is it not an option? What is the critical path, and how do we navigate it without the system freezing up?

Things didn't start out complex, but they sure as heck got that way in the end, partly because of the mechanisms by which lessons were learned and codified.

In 1960, when Kranz was tasked with writing those first mission rules, he literally started with a blank sheet of paper. By 1969, when Apollo 11 launched, things had changed: they worked from a 1,700-page launch plan. Similarly, the approach to rockets had evolved from the early rocket clubs, which took their charges out into a field and lit the fuse, to the Saturn V, which was subjected to every test known to man and then some. In total, each craft underwent 587,500 forms of inspection through its life cycle[24].

When a lesson was learned, it was documented, appropriate procedures were captured and codified and each lesson built upon the last. The effort was additive. By the time Apollo 11 flew, over 30,000 printed pages were needed to check out the vehicle. Rocco Petrone, the launch operations director, said, '*In our testing we had a building block approach, very logical, very methodical; you built each test on the last test, and the whole sequence expanded in the process*'[25].

It's worth noting that the Saturn V was engineered to tolerate failure, built to an engineering reliability target of 99.9%, a pragmatic recognition that failure is always an option. With six million parts, that meant that at every launch, six thousand elements might statistically fail, and still the rocket would fly.

Triple redundancy and an engineering approach that tried to bypass cascade failures meant that in all thirteen missions that Saturn V flew, not one blew up on the launch pad. This was a considerable surprise to all involved.

---

24   *Tests included fire, ice, collision, shock, vibration, dust and rain.*
25   *Quoted in Nelson (2010).*

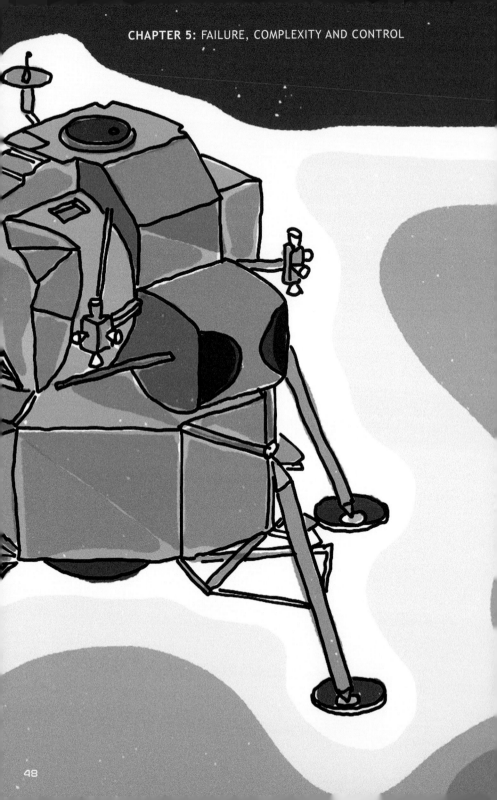

LEADERSHIP
REFLECTIONS

1. **Complexity is engineered and can be additive.** Without the correct webs of sense-making, it can be crippling.

2. Systems are engineered—they do not necessarily operate within a known paradigm. Conversely, **extant systems can trap us within known paradigms**. The context of Apollo gave explicit permission to bring the best of the old, but to create something new.

3. **Creating more noise is easy:** filtering and communicating effectively are the hard parts.

4. **Failure is always an option**, and may be the default state.

NOTES:

CHAPTER 6:
SIMULATION
AND TESTING

There is one discipline that Apollo pursued with remarkable vigour: developing hardware simulators and complex simulations to train and test the astronauts for what might happen and testing their physical and mental prowess to see how prepared they were for the challenge.

In total, the Apollo astronauts spent around a third of their training time in simulators[26]. But all of this testing was in respect of a new domain: nobody was sure quite how the craft would behave, and nobody was certain how a human would stand up to the stresses and strains of space flight.

The technical simulators served two functions: to train astronauts on the correct functioning of systems and collections of systems and to build resilience per the failure of these systems.

Simulations thus tended towards the connected or the dastardly, reflecting the dichotomy at the heart of the training: time on connected simulations allowed an astronaut to rehearse and master every aspect of the mission in sequence, in an environment that as closely mirrored the expected reality as possible. The dastardly simulations tested them in the ways to recover when things went wrong.

But things go wrong in innumerable ways: if the outcome of every simulation was failure, a crash, then that could be both disheartening, and counter-productive. But if every simulation was too easy or predictable, it would add no real resilience, broad capability or learning.

---

26   *I feel sure that this figure was in Morton (2019), but it's on my fact-checking list as I cannot locate it now.*

© Julian Stodd

The role of the SimSup was to design these events, and he would sometimes come under criticism for creating an event so extreme, or unlikely, that it was felt to be unfair. But that is almost the point of failure: certainly failure occurs in known ways, but more often, it's unknown, un-modelled or complex[27]. It's rarely timely or fair.

The Apollo programme required the development of a full range of flight simulators, including General Electric's Spaceflight Visual Simulator[28], which created the world's first visual representation of a landscape on a digital screen.

The Apollo astronauts came to the programme with superlative flight skills, many from the test pilot programme, so all were well accustomed to all manner of aeronautical surprises. The issues they faced, though, was that space flight involves no air once they had left the atmosphere and all the vehicles that they were flying were new—in terms of design and in terms of their sphere of operation.

Both *'fixed base'* and *'moving base'* simulators were created through the Gemini and Mercury programmes. Both could simulate inputs and give some sense of feedback, either through spoofed system inputs and moving images or, in the case of the latter, actually moving the simulation capsule itself.

Alongside the full function simulators were a range of part-task ones that allowed intensive training on one particular aspect of the mission.

In total, Apollo used fifteen different simulators[29] to prepare the astronauts for their missions: three simulated the main Command Module, two were for the Lunar Module that would go to the surface, a Command Module

---

27   This is something that Nassim Nicholas Taleb explores eloquently in his work on Black Swans, and I have previously explored in my own work on Brittle Systems and the limitations of formal hierarchy. https://julianstodd.wordpress.com/2016/05/23/the-limits-of-hierarchy-brittle-systems/ (retrieved 26 July 2019).

28   Morton (2019) provides an interesting review of the speculative historical literature on the lunar experience from before we actually visited the surface.

29   Software became a huge effort for Apollo, with over 350,000 words of programmes and 175 programmers, supported by 200 hardware engineers (in 'Computers in Spaceflight: The NASA Experience', author uncredited).

Procedures part simulator just trained the lunar crew on how to rejoin the Command Module after their landing and the Lunar Module Procedures Simulator just trained the two Moon walkers on procedures of landing and rendezvous.

These simulators were driven by some of the earliest mainframe computers. All of the procedural simulators were run from a single mainframe, while the mission simulators used networks of several mainframes[30]. One challenge that emerged was that the AGC on-board guidance computers for Apollo used a different programming language from the Earth-based DDP-224 simulation mainframes. Developing a functional simulation required twenty experienced IBM programmers and still took around four months to build for each mission. Add that to the six months of training time, and the lag was significant and not able to handle change well.

One analyst, James Raney, thought that things could be done differently. He proposed that instead of recoding the mainframes to try to recreate every instruction on the on-board computers, they could be programmed to run a simulation of the computer itself. Nobody at NASA believed that this *'simulation with a simulation'* approach would work, but in desperation, it was finally approved, and it proved to be a spectacular success[31]. As well as solving an intractable and lengthy problem, Raney's solution cost just $4.6 million, compared to $18 million for the replication approach. It's a great example of a lone voice challenging an established frame of understanding in which the systemic resistance was held more in pride, and existing power structures of the programmers and NASA staff, than it was in evidence or technical issues.

---

30   As above.
31   See 'Computers in Spaceflight: The NASA Experience' for a detailed explanation of the technical dimensions of this, that I won't attempt to replicate.

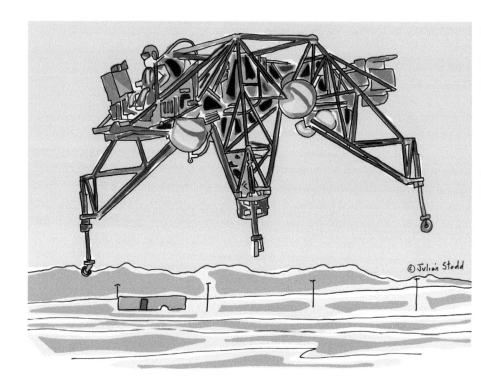

© Julian Stodd

One of the most incredible simulators was the Lunar Landing Research Vehicle, a contraption that looked somewhat like a rocket-powered spider, which used jet engines to support 5/6ths of the vehicle's weight permanently, allowing the pilot to play with the remaining sixth, which should give a reasonable approximation of how the Lunar Module would feel and behave coming in to land.

It was this contraption that nearly killed Neil Armstrong on 6 May 1968, a year before Apollo 11 took off: a propellant leak led to the total loss of control, and with lightning fast reactions, just thirty feet above the ground, Armstrong ejected from the craft, parachuting to safety and avoiding the fireball as the research vehicle exploded. It was not his only brush with death.

Armstrong knew that, in theory at least, the landing computer could manage the entire landing process, bringing them to rest on the Moon's surface without him having to touch a single control. But the test pilot in him was concerned that the sightless machine would land them in a boulder field. Or possibly the test pilot in him could not conceive of missing the opportunity to be the first pilot of a strange craft in a stranger land[32]. The simulators allowed him to develop the vision and approach to handle the varied permutations of this plan. That proved fortuitous when, come the real landing, there was, indeed, a boulder field.

He always intended to take manual control for the last five hundred feet and, in the event the audio tapes of the Eagle landing do not do justice to the zen-like trance and dance occurring between Aldrin (reading out the dwindling fuel level) and Armstrong (unwilling to land between boulders the size of a house and possessing a pilot's instinct that he could clear the field).

Simulation for the Lunar Lander presented an interesting range of frames: flying the lander entirely by hand was perilously risky. Armstrong's preferred approach would be to let the computer handle the throttle while he tilted and tipped the vehicle to influence direction. But there was always the real possibility of a total failure of guidance or control, in which case he would hit the ABORT STAGE button. This would jettison the landing stage and ignite the ascent engine, in itself a risky move because there was no way of knowing how far clear they would be of the discarded bodywork and there would be no time to problem-solve if something went wrong. They could also get back to orbit, but not necessarily anywhere near Collins in the Command Module, a situation that might give them a worse ending that a simple, fiery, glory-filled crash on the surface itself.

Alongside the monumental technology simulation and testing lay the human side of it.

From initial selection through final training, NASA doctors and engineers devised a punishing and, quite frankly, speculative or made up, series of tests. Nobody knew how many g's (one 'g' is the force of gravity we feel

---

32   haikin (1994) provides a great chapter on the simulation of the Moon landings and a perspective on Armstrong's desire to take control.

right now) an astronaut would need to survive. The most extreme roller coasters in the world will subject you to almost 6g. Surprisingly, during launch, an astronaut will only feel a leisurely 3g or so unless things go wrong.

For good measure, NASA developed a centrifuge that spun the astronauts up to 20g, forces that would render the most capable pilot unconscious as their blood drained away from the eyes and brains. The test was unpopular, to say the least.

But it was necessary. On the Gemini 8 flight in 1966, Neil Armstrong and Dave Scott flew to practice rendezvous with an Agena satellite, setting up manoeuvres that would ultimately form part of the Apollo rendezvous mission plan. The early Mercury and Gemini programmes set many of the building blocks in place. But in this instance, a thruster on the Gemini stuck open, and the two mated crafts started to spin. In an effort to control it, Scott threw the switch to separate them, but the now-lighter Gemini started to spin ever faster. Armstrong and Scott fought for survival, until, on the verge of losing consciousness, Armstrong focused and through fading vision was able to isolate the offending thruster.

The testing of the astronauts was not just a matter of spinning: they were probed and prodded in literally every way imaginable. Pre-Apollo, there was some concern about how astronauts would manage the human waste that would be produced. One bright idea was that the best option would be to devise a diet that meant they would produce no waste for ten days. The test subjects in this group described the results on day eleven as traumatic. Not all ideas are good ideas[33].

Much of this human testing was done in the dark: there was little idea of the strains and stresses that would assail a human body in space, so the approach was a mixture of considered planning and wild speculation - a finger in the wind.

---

33 In the end, defecation was handled with plastic bags with adhesive strips. For urination, a condom type attachment to a pipe was needed. In an aside that speaks somewhat to the mentality of astronauts, these caused some problems with leakage in the early days, the condoms being provided in 'small', 'medium', and 'large'. The issue resolved itself when the next batches were labelled 'large', 'extra large' and 'extra extra large'.

LEΛDERSHIP REFLECTIONS

1. **Capability is contextual:** a legacy of success does not guarantee future success.

2. **Testing is only of value if we understand the parameters of operation:** just poking things may be fun, but it is not necessarily valuable.

3. **Split second brilliance probably has a foundation in decades of experience.**

4. **Innovation may occur despite, or in opposition to, the system**, not necessarily nurtured or permitted by it.

5. **Not all brilliant ideas are brilliant: humility is a core trait of leadership.**

6. Simulations can be useful to build specific capability, but **generalised capability is important too.**

NOTES:

CHAPTER 7:
FIRE

Three men died on January 27, 1967. They suffocated in the Command Module of Apollo 1, not in the depths of space or the surface of the Moon, but on Launch Pad 34 at Cape Kennedy, Florida. They died not from an unexpected technical failure or an unknown risk, but rather due to lack of diverse critical thinking and a disconnect between broad knowledge and specific action. They died not because of the unknown, but because of the disconnected.

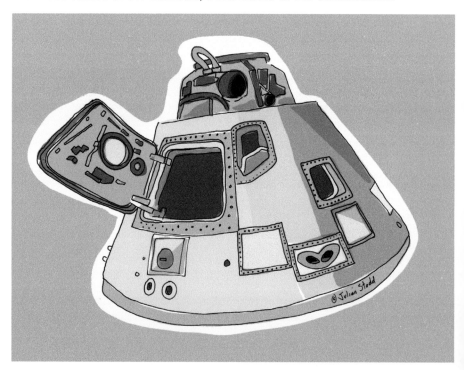

Their deaths, the first US astronauts to die in the American space programme[34], almost halted the race to the Moon, and the lessons learned resonate through the mind-set and approach of NASA to this day[35].

Commander Gus Grissom, veteran Ed White and rookie Roger Chaffee knew that they were not going to the Moon that day. In fact, they knew that they were not going to the Moon at all: the test was of a Command Module called *'Block 1'*, designed as a prototype of the full Command Module, but only to orbit the Earth. Apollo 1 would carry this module into orbit and use the data on its performance to finalise work on *'Block 2'*, currently being finalised by North American, the aerospace company leading on this element. This type of incremental development lay at the heart of the rapid schedule of development that would ultimately deliver success to the programme: the modular nature of the Saturn V and Apollo components and the ability to plug different configurations together meant that sequential testing could be fluid and fast.

Nobody had built a spaceship before, but nonetheless, it was clear to Grissom and his crew that this one had issues. So many changes were being made in the service of different needs and goals that the engineers could barely keep up. The floor of the Command Module was draped with bundles of wire, largely unprotected, constantly getting damaged, and one result of this was that the engineers began to resist the astronauts' suggestions for further change[36]. For the engineers, getting to completion and managing complexity

34 One could argue that a number of test pilots died in precursors of the various modules that ultimately evolved into the Saturn V, and several astronaut candidates died in training accidents, but the Apollo 1 fire was the first in the full-on Apollo programme.
35 Although the lessons resonate, they were arguably not learned. The Challenger Space Shuttle disaster, caused by systems of power and consequence that silenced dissenting voices, had some parallels.
36 This is a key observation in Chaikin (1994) and one that demonstrates how momentum trumped excellence and adaptation, a likely component of the Apollo 1 failure.

may have started to shift focus away from the broader mission objective: to fly a man safely to the Moon and back.

There was a broad perception that this Apollo craft was not just slightly flawed, but downright dangerous. An earlier test of the Service Module engine, the one that would put the craft into lunar orbit, but more importantly that would fire again to send it home, had resulted in the engine nozzle shattering like glass. Indeed, by this stage, the complete vehicle had logged around 20,000 individual failures[37].

Apollo had been preceded by the Gemini programme, during which the astronauts had had regular and welcome input to engineering teams who had seemed part of the crew. But NASA had been smaller then, with less political oversight and pressure. And there was something of a dynastic change. Some felt that the Apollo leaders saw Gemini as quaint and irrelevant, that the mass, momentum and might of Apollo negated the need to learn lessons from its little brother. The hierarchy, system and programme itself bred an arrogance, alongside a systemic disconnect. It was not always clear who could make a final decision, and the expanded teams led to sometimes fragmented pathways. All of this was a recipe for failure.

This particular test was not considered dangerous. The Saturn V was not even fuelled, but when the astronauts first entered it, there was a strong smell of sour milk in the atmosphere, which had taken an hour to resolve. Eventually, the cabin was sealed with the heavy hatch: it came in two parts, with an outer door and an inner frame that opened inwards. And it was a compromise.

Throughout the design, NASA engineers, astronauts and even some engineers at North American had questioned the design, but it had the two key benefits of being light and simple. And as everyone knew, opening inwards meant that, when pressurised in flight, it was far easier to keep an airtight seal. But weight was likely the deciding factor: development of the Apollo modules was substantially a battle against weight, because every single kilo of equipment took dozens of kilos of fuel to heft into orbit.

---

37   Lovell and Kluger (2015) also recount how in an early test of the splashdown, the heat shield had split in two and the $35 million lander had sunk to the bottom of the test tank. This was an inauspicious return to Earth.

Throughout the day, as the three astronauts sweated inside their suits, communications were problematic: the radio links between the Command Module, the Blockhouse and the capsule communicator, were erratic at best. *'Jesus Christ…how are we going to get to the Moon if we can't talk between two or three buildings?'* asked Grissom.

That morning, Grissom and Deke Slayton, chief of crew operations and an astronaut himself, had run through the litany of faults: coolant leaks, faulty wiring, environmental control systems. *'If you don't believe it, you ought to get in there with us'*, said Grissom, an offer that Slayton considered because there would have been space for him to crouch in the equipment bay in his shirt sleeves. But ultimately, he decided he would be better off in the blockhouse, where he could gain a wider view of the test. The decision saved his life, but it haunted him through the rest of his life[38].

At 18:31, an abrupt transmission came from the Command Module: *'Fire'*.

Several hundred meters away, in the Blockhouse, designed to withstand an explosion at launch, Slayton glanced at the black and white monitor that had a camera trained on the exterior of the Command Module: it showed the window in the hatch glowing white, flaring out on the monitor.

A second voice cut in on the radio, in the clear, clipped, tones of a test pilot: *'We've got a fire in the cockpit'*. It was Chaffee, whose role in an emergency was to keep in contact with the Blockhouse.

Slayton could see on the monitor that Ed White was reaching behind and over his head, trying to undo the bolts that held the hatch shut, a futile effort because this required a special tool. *'We've got a bad fire… we're burning up'*, came a more desperate voice. Less than half a minute after that came the final transmission from Apollo one: it was a brief cry of pain.

Outside, the pad technicians fought to get close, but even on the outside, it was too hot: time and again for several minutes, they were beaten back

---

38   *Slayton's own journey is interesting: barred from flight due to a heart irregularity, he sat at the heart of crew operations throughout Apollo before finally being cleared for his own flight in 1975 on the Apollo-Soyuz project.*

by the intense heat. Inside the capsule, in the pure oxygen pressurised atmosphere, even materials that would normally be considered fire-resistant burned with a fierce heat. Velcro, the cargo nets, electrical insulation all exploded into fire, driving temperatures up to over 2,500 Fahrenheit. The huge pressure that built up meant that opening the hatch, a fairly monumental effort even at the best of times, would have been impossible: it was sealed shut with several thousand pounds of force, until the skin of the module itself ruptured after fifteen seconds, venting flames to the outside.

In any event, the astronauts did not burn to death: their air hoses melted in the inferno, and as the cabin ruptured, their breathing apparatus was flooded with carbon monoxide. They lost consciousness between fifteen and thirty seconds and were dead within four minutes.

As the smoke cleared, only blame and sorrow were left behind, both of which lingered for years to come.

Accusations towards North American may have been partly unfounded: the need to save weight was all-consuming, and none of the decisions had been taken without the oversight of NASA. Some of the most damning elements concerned the use of pure oxygen: pure oxygen was used because the complexity of a safer oxygen/nitrogen mix made it prohibitive. In orbit, pure oxygen was necessary, but cabin pressure was only 5psi. On the ground, the cabin was pressurised to 16.7 psi, which was significant. Oxygen is flammable at any pressure, but it becomes terrifyingly flammable at these higher pressures. But nobody questioned why this high pressure was used: it was not necessary for the test, but it had always been done. And an arrogance assumed that all fire risks were correctly managed within the capsule.

The final review board concluded that there had been a spark from damaged wiring on the floor, which ignited vapour from a leaking coolant pipe and then lit the nylon netting (fearsomely flammable in pure oxygen).

In subsequent modules, electrical cables were encased in metal trays to protect the wiring. The amount of Velcro and nylon was reduced, but despite their best efforts, it proved impossible to create a cabin that was fireproof in the enhanced risk of 16psi. Engineer Max Faget came up with a different idea[39]: at launch, the atmosphere would be 60% oxygen to 40% nitrogen, but as the rocket ascended and pressure dropped, they would bleed out the nitrogen until in orbit it was pure oxygen, but at the safe pressure of 5psi. This necessitated protecting the astronauts from getting the bends, like deep-sea divers, so they breathed pure oxygen through their masks the whole way up.

Grissom, Chaffee and White were buried with full military honours, and Pad 34 stands as a monument to their sacrifice. If you visit the Cape, you can take a bus out to it. The plaque reads, *'ad astra per aspera'*[40].
'A rough path leads to the stars'.

When Armstrong and Aldrin finally made it to the surface of the Moon on Apollo 11, Aldrin had a space suit that differed very slightly from the others: in a special pouch, he carried an original mission patch that honoured the three men from Apollo 1 and, in a nice touch, a medal for Soviet cosmonaut Vladimir Komarov, who had died on Soyuz 1, which Aldrin left on the Moon[41].

The effort to get a man to the Moon and return him safely resulted in the construction of the most complex machine ever built by humankind. But the failure of this system came from known risk in a known context: it was not some kind of emergent, radically complex, unknown risk, but rather a pragmatic and clearly visible one, hidden by familiarity and possibly an arrogance of system and design.

Lessons were learned, in part because of the accident that happened on the pad, meaning a full analysis could take place, but the Apollo programme was no longer innocent. The first steps on the Moon had claimed their first price beyond money.

---

39   *Riley and Dolling (2009) provide a useful insight into the entire Apollo 11 hardware setup.*
40   *Nelson (2010) recounts the long struggle that the three widows of the deceased astronauts went through to gain paltry compensation. Ultimately Ed White's wife committed suicide twenty years later while organising a widows' reunion. As I said, the shadows of the failure of the Apollo 1 ran long.*
41   *Recounted in Magnificent Desolation (Aldrin, 2009, p. 3).*

LEADERSHIP REFLECTIONS

1. **Arrogance can be held individually or within a system.**

2. Our knowledge traps us within a frame: **it can be hard to hear weak voices of dissent.**

3. **Risk may sit in plain sight, but it may be normalised.**

4. **The things that 'we have always done' may be the things that we most need to change:** do not assume they are there because of the brilliance of others.

5. **All systems fail:** complexity cannot be infinitely layered.

NOTES:

CHAPTER 8:
SLOWING DOWN

The inferno of lift-off implies that we are trying to leave the Earth, so it seems rather counter-intuitive that a great deal of effort was put into preventing the rocket from doing so: the entire weight of the rocket sat on four hold down arms that prevented the vehicle from moving during transport, but more importantly, prevented it from taking off when the engines fired.

© Julian Stodd

Effectively, the hold-down arms acted like four pincers: left to its own devices, the rocket could shoot off with an erratic and shocking force, especially if, for example, one engine achieved full thrust before the others. Therefore, at launch, all the engines spun up, and once equal thrust was verified, the hold-down arms retracted.

But these arms were not the only thing that held the rocket back: there was a series of controlled release mechanisms, which are best viewed as a series of tapered rods (attached to the rocket) that had to be pulled through a series of discs with holes in them that were attached to the launch pad[42]. The rocket could start to move, but the force required to distort the rods and squeeze them through the holes in the disc again would slow down departure and provide an element of throttling, resulting in a somewhat smoother lift-off.

---

42   *Woods (2016).*

CHAPTER 8: SLOWING DOWN

LEADERSHIP REFLECTIONS

1.   **Pace and tempo count.**

2.   **It's easy to assume that momentum is the answer,** but that is not always correct.

NOTES:

CONCLUSION:

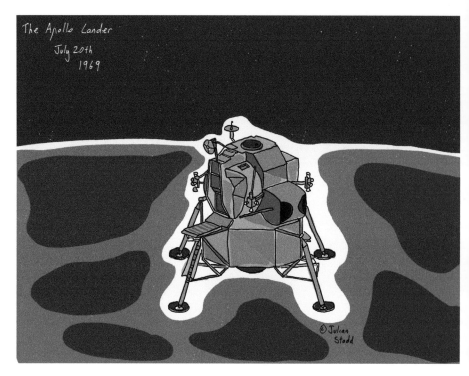

The Apollo Lander
July 20th
1969

© Julian Stodd

It's fifty years since the we landed on the moon: ancient history to some. A story of national achievement and pride to others. Apollo is a story told on many levels: it's the story of the all American hero, a story of technological triumph, or a story of the supremacy of capitalism, depending on the lens you take, or the views that you hold.

In this Guidebook, I have shared the facets of the story that I find most fascinating, inspiring, and insightful, and I have tried to do so through the lens of leadership, and the lessons that we can take forward.

I have tried not to force it, and I hope I was clear from the start: this is not a story that has to be *'complete'*: I do not want the *'lessons'* to be square jawed and rocket powered. I can best describe that I have shared my own reflective space, and hope that you can use these stories to find yours.

THE ILLUSTRATIONS

The illustrations for this book are all drawn on my iPad, using the Paper app, with the exception of the Moonrise image, which is illustrated in silver pen on black cartridge paper, detailed with blue acrylic, and digital highlights on the iPad.

Most images are based on original NASA photography, which I have tried my best to draw.

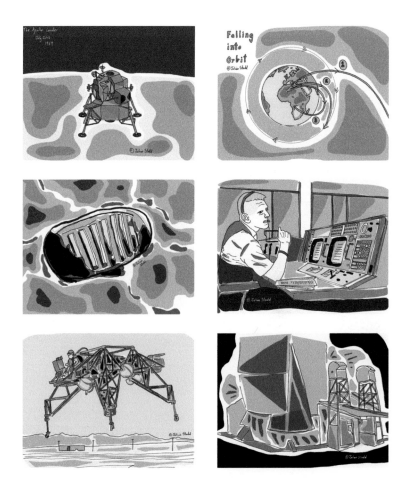

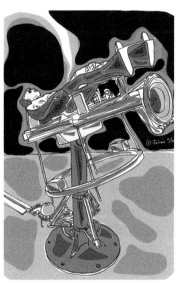

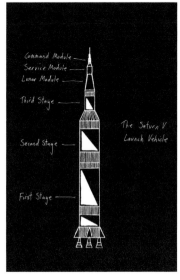

Command Module
Service Module
Lunar Module

Third Stage

Second Stage

First Stage

The Saturn V
Launch Vehicle

ABOUT THE SOCIAL AGE GUIDEBOOKS

The Social Age Guidebooks series is an evolving set of short publications that accompany and compliment my daily work on the blog www.julianstodd.wordpress.com and my longer form work that is published as full books.

The guidebooks are all around 10,000 words and share work that is research-based, but still evolving. When possible, I try to keep them practical and applied, although in this case, unless you are heading to the Moon, it's a little more reflective.

An important principle of the Social Age Guidebooks is also that they are all free, as is my work on the blog. This is central to an approach of #WorkingOutLoud, to which I subscribe. Because of production costs, I have to sell my complete books, but I am proud of this series that I can give away.

All of the guidebooks are available for purchase in paperback if you wish to have the artefact, but they are free online.

Crucially, they do not contain your answers: they contain mine.

The context of the Social Age, which contextualises all of my work, is that it is a time of constant change. Only through curiosity, humility and our engaged communities can we find a way to adapt.

I will draw and share my own sketch map, but all I can do is share it in the hope that it helps you draw yours.

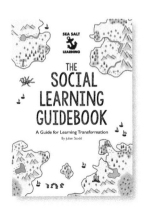

The Social Learning Guidebook

This short Social Learning Guidebook is intended to highlight areas that you should consider when you look at learning transformation. It is not intended to have all the answers, but rather to offer some frameworks and models that you may want to adopt, and include activities that you can do along the way.

www.seasaltlearning.com/the-social-learning-guidebook/

The Community Builder Guidebook

The Community Builder Guidebook is an exploration of *'Communities'*, and the key capabilities of Social Leaders and Community Builders. As with other books in this Guidebook series, Julian offers thoughtful exploration of the topic, along with a practical guide of how to do it. The 9 chapters support you to build new communities as well as help existing ones to thrive and grow.

www.seasaltlearning.com/the-community-builder-guidebook/

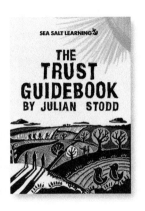

The Trust Guidebook

In this Guidebook, Julian Stodd leads the reader through 12 aspects of the *'Landscape of Trust'*, exploring the best ways to understand it, and to share stories as we go. Through this, we find out how to lead, and to engage with Trust.

This is an accompanying Guidebook to Julian's *'The Trust Sketchbook'*, also available from Sea Salt Publishing.

www.seasaltlearning.com/the-trust-guidebook

BIBLIOGRAPHY AND FURTHER READING

Aldrin, Buzz (2009): *'Magnificent Desolation: the long journey home from the moon'*. Bloomsbury, London.

Brzezinski, Matthew (2007): *'Red Moon Rising: Sputnik and the rivalries that ignited the Space Age'*. Bloomsbury Publishing, London.

Chaikin, Andrew (1994): *'A man on the Moon: the voyages of the Apollo Astronauts'*. Penguin, London.

'Computers in Spaceflight: the NASA Experience - Chapter Nine - Making New Reality: Computers in Simulations and Image Processing' https://history.nasa.gov/computers/Ch9-2.html (Retrieved 25th July 2019)

Day, Dwayne (2006): *'Saturn's fury: effects of a Saturn 5 launch pad explosion'*. http://www.TheSpaceReview.com (retrieved 23rd July 2019) http://www.thespacereview.com/article/591/1

Hadfield, Chris (2013): *'An astronauts guide to life on Earth'*. Macmillan, London.

Hadfield, Chris (2014): *'You are here: around the world in 92 minutes'*. Pan Books, London.

Kranz, Gene (2000): *'Failure is not an option: Mission Control from Mercury to Apollo 13 and beyond'*. Simon and Schuster, New York.

Kelly, Thomas (2001): *'Moon Lander: how we developed the Apollo lunar module'*. Smithsonian Books, USA.

Lovell, James, and Kluger, Jeffrey (2015): *'Apollo 13'*. Hodder and Stoughton, London.

Mailer, Norman, (2009): *'Moonfire'*. Taschen, Germany.

Morton, Oliver (2019): *'The Moon'*. Profile Books, London.

Muir-Harmony, Teasel and Collins, Michael (2018): *'A history in 50 objects - Apollo to the moon'*. National Geographic, Washington DC.

Nelson, Craig (2010): *'Rocket Men: the epic story of the first men on the moon'*. John Murray, London.

Riley, Christopher, and Woods, David, and Dolling, Philip (2012): *'Lunar Rover: 1971-1972 (Apollo 15-17; LRV1-3 & 1G Trainer)'*. Haynes Publishing, Yeovil.

Riley, Christopher, and Dolling, Phil (2009): *'NASA Mission AS506, Apollo 11, 1969 (including Saturn V, CM-107, SM-107, LM-5), Owners' Workshop Manual'*. Haynes, Yoevil.

Stodd, Julian (2016): *'The Limits of Hierarchy - Brittle Systems'*. https://julianstodd.wordpress.com/2016/05/23/the-limits-of-hierarchy-brittle-systems/ retrieved 26th July 2019

Woods, David (2016): *'NASA Saturn V, 1967-1973 (Apollo 4 to Apollo 17 & Skylab), Owners' Workshop Manual'*. Haynes, Yeovil.

THE '100 DAY', & 'SKETCHBOOK', SERIES

Whilst *'Handbooks'* and *'Guidebooks'* are about ideas and strategy, the *'100 Day'* books tackle how we do these things at scale. They do so by providing a scaffolded space, which you can explore, document, and graffiti, as you go.

'Social Leadership: My First 100 Days' is a practical, guided, reflective journey. It follows 100 days of activity, with each day including provocations, questions, and actions. You fill in the book as you go. It's accompanied by a full set of 100 podcasts.

'The Trust Sketchbook' is another guided, reflective journey, a walk through the Landscape of Trust, but in this case you graffiti and adapt the book, to capture your own landscape.

OTHER BOOKS

I have written a series of other books, covering aspects of learning, culture, technology, and knowledge, which you can find details of on the blog.

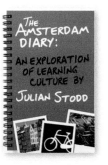

CERTIFICATIONS

In 2018 I launched the first Certification programme on *'Storytelling in Social Leadership'*. It's based upon *'Foundations'* and *'Techniques'*, which are practical and applied, and *'Experiments'*, which you learn to run in your own Organisation.

Throughout 2019 and 2020, the Certification offering is growing rapidly to include:

'Storytelling in Social Leadership' *'Modern Learning Capabilities'*
'Leading with Trust' *'Leading Through Change'*
'Community Building' *'Social Age Navigation'*
'Foundations of Social Leadership' Get in touch to find out more.

MOOCS AND PODCASTS

I run two MOOCs, one on *'Foundations of the Social Age'*, and one to accompany *'Social Leadership: My First 100 Days'*. You can find details at www.seasaltlearning.com, or drop me a line.

I publish occasional podcasts, on all aspects of my work. You can find me through your usual podcast player.

THE BLOG AND THE CAPTAIN'S LOG

I write the blog every day, sharing my current thinking and illustrations. You can find it at www.julianstodd.wordpress.com

I write a weekly newsletter for Social Age Explorers: it comments on news items, from the perspective of the Social Age, as well as providing expanded commentary around my own writing and thinking.
Visit www.bit.ly/TheCaptainsLog to sign up.

SEA SALT LEARNING

In a more formal space, I founded Sea Salt Learning in 2014, acting as a global partner for change. We help some of the biggest and most interesting Organisations in the world get fit for the Social Age, through strategic consulting, building capability in teams, and building programmes to reach out at scale.

THE SOCIAL LEADERSHIP HANDBOOK

The Social Leadership Handbook provides a foundational view of reputation based authority, and explores how we build and share this type of power.

Social Leadership encapsulates the mindset, skills and behaviours required to be an effective leader in the Social Age.

It recognises that power and authority are founded more on what you curate and share, how you build your reputation, than simple positional authority.

It's a model of leadership that is more fluid and relevant than ones based on longevity, situation or hierarchy. Under a social model, sharing and narrating trump command and control.

It's a collaborative venture with communities at it's heart.

The NET Model of Social Leadership is built around three Dimensions: *'Narrative'*, *'Engagement'* and *'Technology'*. The NET model is both an idea and a call to arms.

This book is a guide for organisations looking to develop Social Leadership capability and for individuals looking to become Social Leaders.